CARINE MACKENZIE
Illustrated by Angelo Ruta

THE PROMISE

How God Told the World about JESUS

The Promise

How God Told the World about Jesus

You have probably made lots of promises, but have you always kept them? Probably not.

When God makes a promise, he keeps it. In the Old Testament he promised that he would send a Saviour. The Saviour would forgive the sins of those who trusted in him. He would defeat Satan, the evil one. God planned this before the world began.

Although the promise took many years to be fulfilled, at just the right time, God sent the Saviour, his own beloved Son, to the earth to live and die and rise again from the dead.

God told several men through the centuries about his promise and by faith they believed what God said. Let's find out about some of these people.

ADAM AND EVE (GENESIS 3)

When God made Adam and Eve, the first man and woman, he wanted them to worship and obey him. 'Eat from any tree,' God said, 'except the tree of the knowledge of good and evil in the middle of the garden. If you eat from that tree, you will die.'

But, Satan, disguised as a serpent, deceived Eve. She disobeyed God. She ate the fruit and gave some to Adam. Sin entered the world. Adam and Eve were no longer perfect.

God has to punish sin. He is perfectly holy. However, he gave Adam and Eve hope for the future. God told the serpent, 'The woman's son will crush your head and you will hurt his heel.'

This was the first hint that God gave of his promise of a Saviour. Jesus Christ fulfilled this promise when he died on the cross, saving his people from sin, defeating Satan and death.

NOAH (GENESIS 6-8)

Noah lived with his family in a way that pleased God. But all the other people did not care about God. They lived sinful, violent lives. God decided to destroy these wicked people with a great flood. He told Noah to build a boat so that he and his family, and every kind of animal, bird and creature that crept along the ground would be safe when the flood came.

When the waters receded, the boat – called an ark – came to a stop on Mount Ararat. Noah left the ark several weeks later. His first act was to worship God.

God made a special promise (called a covenant) with Noah and his sons. 'Never again will I destroy all living creatures with a flood.' As a sign of the promise, God put a rainbow in the sky.

Noah found safety from God's anger by obeying God's Word and going into the ark. If we obey God's Word and repent and trust in Jesus, he will be a safe place for us and will protect us from God's righteous anger.

ABRAHAM AND SARAH (GENESIS 12-18)

Abraham and Sarah lived in Mesopotamia. One day, God told Abraham, 'Leave your father's house, and go to the land that I will show you.'

God made a promise to Abraham. 'I will make your family into a great nation. I will bless you. All the peoples in the world will be blessed through you.' By faith, Abraham obeyed and went on the long journey to the land of Canaan.

This promise pointed to one of Abraham's descendants – forty-two generations later – Jesus Christ. We might think that is a long time to wait for a promise to be fulfilled, but God's timing is perfect.

One day, Abraham saw three men approaching. These were no ordinary visitors. The Lord had come with a message, 'This time next year, Sarah will have a son.' Sarah, listening out of sight, laughed. How could that be possible when she and Abraham were so old? 'Why did Sarah laugh?' the Lord said, 'Is anything too hard for the Lord?' Sarah was afraid. 'I did not laugh,' she said. But the Lord cannot be deceived. 'You did laugh,' he replied.

A year later, Sarah had a son, Isaac. Abraham believed that God would keep his promise of sending a Saviour to the world. Jesus himself spoke about Abraham centuries later, '... Abraham rejoiced that he would see my day. He saw it and was glad' (John 8:56). Abraham knew by faith that God's promised Saviour would come to the world.

ABRAHAM AND ISAAC (GENESIS 22, JOHN 1:29)

One day, God said to Abraham, 'Take Isaac, whom you love, to Mount Moriah. There you will sacrifice him as an offering.'

Abraham believed that God could raise Isaac from the dead, if he wished. He obeyed God faithfully.

Isaac carried the wood and Abraham took the knife and the fire. 'Where is the lamb for the offering?' Isaac asked.

'God will provide a lamb,' Abraham replied.

After Abraham built the altar, and tied Isaac to it, he raised the knife ready to kill his son. The angel of the Lord called out, 'Do not harm the boy! I know that you fear God, because you were willing to sacrifice your only son, Isaac.'

Then Abraham saw a ram caught in a bush. The ram was used as the sacrifice – not a lamb. Centuries later, God did provide a lamb as a sacrifice for sin. 'Behold the Lamb of God,' John the Baptist said about Jesus. God did not spare his own Son, but offered him up as a sacrifice for sin.

ISAAC AND JACOB (GENESIS 26, 28)

When Isaac was living in the land of Gerar, God appeared to him. 'I will bless you and your children. Through your offspring all the nations of the earth shall be blessed.'

This same promise was repeated to Jacob, Isaac's son. One night he was sleeping outside with a stone for a pillow. He had a dream where he saw a ladder reaching up to heaven and angels of God were ascending and descending on it. The Lord spoke from heaven, 'Through you and your children shall all the families of the earth be blessed. I am with you and will keep you wherever you go.'

Early in the morning, Jacob took the stone that had been his pillow and set it up as a pillar and poured oil on it. He named that place Bethel, which means 'house of God'.

MOSES (EXODUS 7–12)

God told Moses to lead his people out of Egypt where they were slaves to Pharaoh. Pharaoh did not want to let them go. God sent plagues on the Egyptians as punishment. The final plague meant the death of the eldest son in each family. However, the Hebrew people followed God's special instructions. They killed a lamb and sprinkled its blood on the doorposts and lintels of their houses. When the angel of death passed through Egypt, he passed over the houses marked with blood.

A meal of roast lamb was eaten before they left Egypt. This Passover meal was held every year from then on, reminding the people of God's promise. It pointed them to the promised Saviour, Jesus Christ, who would shed his blood on the cross so that his people would escape eternal death.

DAVID (1 & 2 SAMUEL, MARK 10)

David, King of Israel, composed many Psalms, and some of them referred to the coming Messiah, the Lord Jesus Christ. When he spoke about the king, he did not mean himself or any other earthly king. He was referring to the King of kings, the Lord Jesus. 'Your throne, O God, is forever and ever. The sceptre of your kingdom is a sceptre of uprightness' (Psalm 45:6 ESV).

David was one of Jesus' ancestors. One day, a blind beggar called out to Jesus for help. 'Jesus, Son of David, have mercy on me!' When Jesus rode into Jerusalem, on his way to die on the cross, the crowd shouted in praise to him, 'Hosanna to the Son of David!'

THE OLD TESTAMENT PROPHETS

God's message through the prophet, Isaiah, tells us that the Messiah's mother would be a virgin.

Jeremiah told of the coming king who would reign wisely and do what is just and right. He would be called, 'The Lord our Righteousness'.

Micah foretold that this king would be born in Bethlehem.

Zechariah spoke about the coming king who would be humble, riding on a donkey.

Daniel told of a vision he had of one like a son of man. He was given authority and glory and power. People of every nation would worship him. Only the Lord Jesus Christ could match this amazing description.

All through Old Testament times, God was preparing his people for the coming Saviour. His promise was being revealed bit by bit.

In God's own time, the Saviour, the Son of God, came to the world.

MARY AND JOSEPH (MATTHEW 1, LUKE 1)

Mary was a young woman from Nazareth, in Israel. One day, an angel gave her startling news.

'You are going to have a baby boy. You will call his name Jesus. He will be great and will be called the Son of the Most High. The Lord God will give him the throne of his father David, and he will reign over the house of Jacob forever: his kingdom will never end.'

'How can this happen,' said Mary, 'since I am a virgin?'

'The baby is the Son of God. You will have this child by the power of God, the Holy Spirit', replied the angel.

When Mary's fiancé, Joseph, heard that she was expecting a baby, he was unhappy. But in a dream he heard an angel say, 'Do not be afraid to take Mary as your wife. The child she is expecting is the Son of God. You shall call his name Jesus, for he will save his people from their sins.'

Because of a special census, Joseph, along with his wife Mary, had to go to Bethlehem, his home town. It was there that Mary's baby was born – fulfilling the prophecy of Micah long before.

ANGELS AND SHEPHERDS (LUKE 2)

In fields near Bethlehem, shepherds were watching over their sheep. Suddenly, an angel appeared. They were terrified.

'Don't be afraid,' the angel said. 'I bring good news for you and all the people. Today, a Saviour has been born in Bethlehem. He is Christ the Lord. If you go now, you will find the baby in a manger.'

Suddenly, a crowd of angels praised God saying, 'Glory to God in the highest! Peace and good will to all people!'

The shepherds found Mary, Joseph and the baby, just as the angels had told them. They passed on the good news to everyone they met.

Abraham and Isaac and Jacob had been promised that one of their descendants would be a blessing to the whole world. The shepherds were told that this special person had been born that day in Bethlehem. What wonderful news!

SIMEON (LUKE 2)

Some time later, Mary and Joseph took the baby Jesus to the temple to present him to the Lord. There they met a man called Simeon, a holy man who loved the Lord. God had promised him that he would not die until he had actually seen the promised Saviour.

When Simeon saw Jesus, he knew that God's promise had come to pass. 'I am ready to die,' he said, 'for I have seen God's salvation.'

Simeon told Mary that her son would be rejected by many in Israel, but would be the greatest joy to many others.

'A sword will pierce your own soul too,' he said to Mary – hinting at the grief she would experience when Jesus came to die.

Jesus grew up in Nazareth, living a perfect sinless life like no other person.

JOHN THE BAPTIST (LUKE 3)

One day, John the Baptist saw Jesus and said to the people around, 'Look, the Lamb of God, who takes away the sin of the world.'

Do you remember what Abraham said to Isaac on Mount Moriah? 'God will provide a lamb.' God did provide the lamb in his own Son, the Lord Jesus Christ.

One day, Jesus asked the disciples, 'Who do you say I am?' Peter answered, 'You are the Christ, the Son of the Living God.'

'My Father in heaven has taught you that,' replied Jesus.
From then on, Jesus warned his disciples that he would suffer greatly and die. This would not be a defeat, but the great work of salvation for his people. This was why Jesus came into the world.

THE LORD'S SUPPER (LUKE 19, 22 & 23)

Jesus knew what was ahead of him, yet he did not shirk from his task. He went ahead to Jerusalem, riding on a donkey as Zechariah had said.

He ate the Passover meal with his disciples in an upstairs room. When he broke the bread, he said, 'This is my body, broken for you.' He passed round the cup of wine, saying, 'This is my blood. When you eat the bread and drink the wine, remember me.' We call this the Lord's Supper. Followers of Jesus all over the world still remember him in this way.

After being betrayed by Judas, Jesus was arrested. Remember that Simeon had told Mary that many would reject her son. Even Peter, Jesus' friend and disciple, denied three times that he knew Jesus.

Jesus was sent to Pilate, the Roman governor, then to King Herod. He was mocked and then sent back to Pilate. Weakly Pilate gave in to public opinion and he sent Jesus to be crucified.

THE CROSS (LUKE 23, JOHN 19)

Jesus was nailed to a wooden cross, but he was not angry. 'Father, forgive them,' he said, 'for they do not realise what they are doing.' He suffered alone. Even God his Father abandoned him. Jesus took the punishment for the sins of his people – all those who trust in him from the past, the present and the future.

How painful all of this must have been for Mary, Jesus' mother. It must have been like a sword piercing her soul – just as Simeon had said.

However, all this was in God's plan that Jesus, God's Son, should die to save his people from their sins.

Early in the morning of the first day of the week, some ladies came to the tomb where Jesus was buried. They wanted to anoint the body with spices. 'Who will roll the stone away for us?' they wondered.

But the stone was already rolled away and an angel was sitting on it. Inside the tomb, an angel said to them, 'Do not be afraid. I know you are looking for Jesus. Do not look for him here. He is risen from the dead.'

Mary Magdalene wept in the garden. She did not know what had happened to Jesus. She spoke to a man who she thought was the gardener. The man spoke her name, 'Mary', and she immediately realised that he was Jesus.

Mary ran with the good news to the disciples. In the days that followed, all the disciples and over 500 people saw Jesus risen from the dead.

THE ASCENSION (MATTHEW 28, LUKE 24)

Jesus gave his disciples a special work to do. 'Go and make disciples of all nations, baptising them in the name of the Father, and of the Son and of the Holy Spirit. Teach these disciples to obey all the commands I have given you.'

Jesus then raised his hands to bless them and he was lifted up into heaven, through the clouds. The astonished disciples gazed into the sky.

Two men in white clothes stood beside them. 'Why are you standing there staring? Just as you have seen Jesus being taken up into heaven, he will return to earth one day.'

Joyfully, the disciples went to work with energy, praising God and preaching his Word everywhere they went.

This good news has come to you too.

The promised Saviour was born and lived a perfect life. He died to save his people from their sins. He conquered death by rising from the grave. He ascended into heaven where he is continually praying for his people. He sent the Holy Spirit to be with his people to help and guide them, and one day he will return.

What an amazing promise! What an amazing Saviour!
All God's promises are fulfilled perfectly in Jesus Christ.

Christian Focus Publications publishes books for adults and children under its four main imprints: Christian Focus, Christian Heritage, CF4K and Mentor. Our books reflect that God's word is reliable and Jesus is the way to know him, and live for ever with him.

Our children's publication list includes a Sunday school curriculum that covers pre-school to early teens; puzzle and activity books. We also publish personal and family devotional titles, biographies and inspirational stories that children will love.

If you are looking for quality Bible teaching for children then we have an excellent range of Bible story and age specific theological books. From pre-school to teenage fiction, we have it covered!

Find us at our web page: www.christianfocus.com

10 9 8 7 6 5 4 3 2 1
Copyright © 2016 Carine Mackenzie
Christian Focus Publications
ISBN: 978-1-78191-619-3
Published by Christian Focus Publications,
Geanies House, Fearn, Tain, Ross-shire,
IV20 1TW, Scotland, U.K.

Cover design by Daniel van Stratten
Illustrations by Angelo Ruta
Printed in China

CF4 •K
*Because you're never
too young to know Jesus*